JUST ANOTHER TUESDAY

poems and reflections

REBECCA ALMEIDA

Just Another Tuesday
Copyright © 2025 Rebecca Almeida

Produced and printed by Stillwater River Publications.
All rights reserved. Written and produced in the United States of America.
This book may not be reproduced or sold in any form without the expressed, written permission of the author(s) and publisher.

Visit our website at
www.StillwaterPress.com
for more information.

First Stillwater River Publications Edition

ISBN: 978-1-968548-12-4

1 2 3 4 5 6 7 8 9 10

Written by Rebecca Almeida.
Published by Stillwater River Publications,
West Warwick, RI, USA.

*The views and opinions expressed
in this book are solely those of the author(s)
and do not necessarily reflect the views
and opinions of the publisher.*

This collection of poetry and reflections is dedicated to my kids, my loves, my inspirations, and my challenges.

Also, my family and friends. My fellow warrior mamas, advocates and people who are trying to navigate through this journey of life with added challenging blessings.

The incredible drawings that are scattered throughout the poems were drawn and created by some pretty amazing kids with superpowers! Different abilities are awesome and should be celebrated, highlighted and shared! I am so thankful to each one of my fantastic young artists!

As we all walk through our journeys, we are met with blessings and joy, obstacles and challenges. No matter what,

You are not alone!

This book was written as an outlet for processing emotions, celebrations, feelings of pain, sometimes inadequacies. It is meant to educate some and encourage other families through this journey.

Some of the material is raw emotion. Please be aware as you read that some may be triggering.

It is meant to bring healing, awareness and freedom!

Much love as you read!

Becky

Contents

Just Another Tuesday! 1
My Inspirations 13
Mama's Heart 43
Children's Mental Health 83
Children's Behavioral Health 133
Letters 143
Addiction 149
Grief 159
Sickness 179
Sexual Abuse 185

A Note from the Author *197*

1

Just Another Tuesday!

Just Another Tuesday!

I think we need a bubble
To hide us away
To protect all of us
Each and every day
From prostate cancer
To sinus trouble
From CIDP
And major depression
To arthritis and anxiety
ADHD, bipolar disorder
Autism is another in our family tree
Hernias and ear tubes,
Need reductions of our boobs
Weight loss and weight gain
Shoulder, knee, and hip pain
Needing MiraLAX
Trouble going potty
Probably because we can't relax
MRIs and CT scans
Big pull ups and bed pans
Surgery seems like a regular day
ER visits. oh, it's Tuesday!
A laundry list of things on and on
Kidney cancer
Ostomy bag
Trouble on the john
Tonsillitis, ear infections
Can't make up this crazy
Some really try hard

While some, really lazy
Hearing loss, reflux, developmental delay, behavioral issues, rehabs, just another day.
Auto immune disorders
Pain all the time nothing makes any sense
No reason, no rhyme
Appointments take over
Running around
Can't get away from the chaos
And all the Crazy sound
From alcohol and drug addiction
Suffering from serious affliction
Mental health issues detected
Generational curses
So many affected
Gut wrenching perversion
Severing relationships
Creating aversion
Selfishness, maybe, unaware
Taking advantage
Unfair
Abuse
Of any form
Every day
another storm! —

Outreach Or?

It's all well and good to sit there in a pew
to have all of those
outreaches
but between me and you,
The lights and the fancy whistles and the giant bell
The fellowships, the outreach to people you think are headed for hell.
Yet here we sit watching service from here
We can't bring our families because of our fear
But wait, don't judge that
Until you hear what I have to say
Our children have severe needs and cannot handle Sunday.
Autism is hard and steals much
From sensitivity to lights and sounds
To being Frightened by touch
Angry outbreaks when nobody knows why
Then there are times they just tantrum
then sit there and cry.
Other times they check out of their mind
Can't seem to reach them
We cannot seem to find
A way to settle their little raging heart
Coping skills, deep breaths, back to the start
We pray we ask for pastors and elders to come
We leave messages and voicemails
Please can you pray for my son.
Please remember we all can't be in that place
We can't be part of the service
You can't see my face
You don't know the tears or the cries of my heart

There are thousands like me
Whose is reaching out and
Making us part?
I try not to be bitter, I try not to get mad, when I reach out for someone to pray with me...
SILENCE... makes me sad! —

Our Story

When someone hears our story
They think it can't be true
How can so many crazy things
Keep happening to you
When someone hears our story
How do you do it, they say
There are no other options
There is no other way
When someone hears our story
They tell us we must want to quit
We look at them and smile
And respond with quick wit
When someone hears our story
They try to offer a hand
But when we really need it
Alone is where we stand
When someone hears our story
We are not the only one
To live with all the madness
Our day has just begun
When someone hears our story
Nobody knows what to do
Just being there to hear our story
Helps our minds renew
So, when you hear of a family
About to lose their mind
The struggles are so difficult
Good friends are hard to find.—

The Coffee Shop

The smell of coffee brewing
The pastry in the case
The people behind the counter
Bring a smile to my face
Some say it's different
When greeted with a hello
Nowadays it's not normal
To feel so welcomed when you go
The spectrum of abilities
The acceptance look and see
They don't see disability
Everyone is treated equally
This place is somewhere
For so many talents too shine
A Handmade gift made specially
Each individual, a special design
The world is made up of so many unique people
Everyone has their own differences
Celebrating each one
Not based on appearances
But look at the heart
And the love put in
Look at the person
Humanity begins!—

Thank you to Red,White and Brew!
www.redwhitebrewri.com

Artist is Connor, age 5

Hallways

This hallway is filled with so many people
Some angry, some confused, some lonely
Waiting to see what the judge will say
Some sit, some pace, most play on their phones making time pass feeling alone
No eye contact made between this woman or man
Not much being said except arguing about a plan.
Why is it like this nobody seems to care
Lost lonely people who knows everywhere
What happened to him to make him so sad
Why is her heart broken? Her life must have been bad
Here we all sit outside of the courtroom.
All different reasons
All different stories
All different outcomes
All different worries
People are here young middle aged and old,
So many with empty eyes
So many so cold
It's really quite sad here in this long hallway
It's really not a place you want to spend your day!—

2

My Inspirations

BEST LADY

October 25, 1921, the world became a better place. This was the day that the birth of a baby girl named Dorothy entered this world! Known by everyone as Toppy, she was a daughter, a sister, a friend, an aunt, a nurse, a wife, mother, a mother-in-law, a grandmother, a great-grandmother, a great-great-grandmother, a hero to many, a true gem to us all!

I am going to tell you about my Gamma, not only was she my grandmother, but she was also my most cherished friend. I could call her at any time, and she never failed to be on the other end to hear my jokes, wise comebacks, which mind you were usually followed by her infectious laugh, a REBECCA, and yet another giggle and sometime even a snort! She also gave wise counsel and helped me navigate through many tough days!

I was her Becca... not just anyone could call me that and she was the only one who got to call me Becca poo!

Growing up I remember sleep overs on Lunn St. Gam hosting me and Lance and Kristen. We would play hide and seek... hiding in the ceramic studio. We would look at all the molds and clay figurines just waiting to be painted.

I know I cherish those memories! The ceramics class with all the ladies gathered around the long table in the basement, and my Gamma telling us all what to do. Yes, she let me sneak in on many a class and learn to paint like her!

I remember one time; I was painting a giant minnie mouse. The class had several of the regulars all seated and the smells of the room are still fresh in my mind. Clay, paint, glaze and the certain sweet smell of my Gamma! Anyway, I was scraping the edges off where the mold left a line all around. As I went around the face, the little tool pulled the nose right off minnie... I, being the silly kid, was holding the nose of Minnie.

I dipped it in water and stuck it to the end of my nose! Well, I think my Gamma and Dot Brown almost peed their pants with laughter... tears of joy and snorts lasted for a while, and we just had fun!

The other side of that is she said this ... give it to me, and I will fix it! Well, that without her even realizing set an example of what she truly was! Taking Minnie's nose and getting the wet clay, mending the nose and making sure it was ready to be painted into something beautiful.

She was always there to help rebuild, encourage and make something broken look beautiful! She made me always feel like I was the most important person to her. She made everyone feel that way! What a gift that was!!

Trips to Disney, and long rides to her beloved York State... driving in the back of the white Ford Tempo, WLKW classical music playing in the car... her and Gram in the front seat and me... in the back ... the smell of Canada Mints permeating my nose, the endless scene of trees as we drove 5 hours to see Flora, Barney and Janet. The music to this day for me is known as car sick music...lol I remember thinking we would never arrive and that music would never end!

Saturday nights, sitting on the little red stool in front of her, with the back of my shirt up and her crooked nails, which mind you scratched better than any... ever!!! ... scratch my back while we all were "entertained" by the bubbles and dancing and car sick music of the late great Lawrence Welk Show! Thankfully it was only a 30-minute show, and we would wait as the Wonderful World of Disney movie would follow! What I wouldn't give for another time to watch Bobby & Sissy waltz around while my back was being scratched!

I remember when I was in fourth grade, and we moved in with Gamma and Gram on Lunn St. I was the lucky one who shared a room with her! I had one twin bed, and she had the other. It was so nice sleeping near her and opening my eyes at the crack of dawn (usually because Gram was dust mopping and trying to get our sheets to wash at 5 am. It didn't matter that we were still half asleep) but I could look across the room and see my Gamma right there! Such a sense of love and comfort!

Then there was the bathroom off the bedroom. My brother Justin and I were just joking about the blue water so Calgon could take us away. That stuff made her tub awesome! We could climb our behinds up the slope in the tub, balance our biscuits and slide down into the water... though it may have been 2 feet, to us it felt like a fun water ride!

The glass jar with the powder puff, is always an appetizing source of cloudy fun to poof powder all over after getting out of our water ride! Such happy times!

As we grew older and Gamma and Gram moved on to the "Rog"... Roger Williams Ave. where the ceramics studio became a new location and fun place. Now add the smells of laundry soap and fabric softener to the clay and glaze! Still painting... and doing her "washin"

At one point we became neighbors! That was a special time for me. We shared things... I would cook... (she usually said too much Rebecca, this is enough for 3 meals) and she loved to do the laundry. She was the best!

One day she decided she was going to cook dinner for us; my son Zack was about 3. She made us a pot of beef stew. We all know cooking was not her strength! Well Zack took a bite of the soup and chewed. He chewed and chewed some more. Finally, he looked at me and smiled and said.... Mmmmmmm Amma made Gum soup! This always made us all laugh! But can we talk about the lemon squares??? I think we all would secretly try to be the one to steal the pan of lemon squares and hide it, we Loved those!!!! By the way... Rachael never knew there was such a thing because Justin and I always got to them first! Oh and....I have the recipe! Though they will never quite taste quite like hers!

I have heard stories throughout the 49 plus years I have been blessed to be loved by her. I have learned that I didn't lick stubborn off a tree, and I didn't get my independent nature from under a rock! While these qualities can be used for not good things. My Gamma chose to use them for amazing things!

WWII ARMY nurse Lt. she is a brave hero always... saving lives and risking her own! She was so humble about this and never really shared the magnitude of her experiences until she was asked to do the documentary! My Gamma ... Our Hero!

A daughter, selfless, loving and giving. I watched her take care of Gram until she couldn't anymore. From Maalox to prunes and honey dew melons. to fasten the corset that to this day baffles me of how that could have possibly been comfortable! She was a true example of what a daughter should be!

A mother; proud, loving, encouraging looking at her 3 girls with such a sparkle in her eyes! Mom, Aunties, you made her the Mommy she was. You gave her the love and respect and upheld her in Highest honor even after her last breath!

A mother-in-law: never once did I ever hear a bad thing said about her sons-in-law, she loved them so much and they loved her just as much!

A grandmother: we as her grandchildren were so blessed! She loved each and every one of us, never forgetting a birthday for any of us! Always giving and never expecting anything in return except our love which we gladly poured into her and she into us!

A great grandmother: the pride she had in Each of you as you were the ones as Gramps said, "made her great", we all knew she was beyond great!!! Keep making her proud as she is smiling down on you!

A great great grandmother. Not many get to this stage of life, but she did! Many rise and call her blessed! Walk everyday knowing how much she loves you!

An Aunt; so, so many stories of Aunt Toppy! I loved hearing them. Still do! She had such a huge heart That always had room for everyone!

A sister: you know one thing that always made me smile so much was the relationship I saw between my Gamma and her siblings! Aunt Jonsie ... Norma... she would say to us ... boy did she hold you so high in her heart!!! I hope I can be even half the sister you both were to each other! And Uncle Jeff, her baby brother... she loved you so much. Then Uncle Bud, I remember times at the Rog, when he and Aunt Dottie would visit and they would talk for hours! True example of love!

A friend: Everyone could always count on my Gamma. Whether it was to clip coupons, save box tops, save shopping bags, give to causes close to her heart or just be there to be an ear or a shoulder, or the best thing was her arms to hug! I remember her wearing a Button she wore so proudly as she loved to give hugs! One day, she thought she was sporting her advertisement for being a hug therapist... I said to her, Gam, did you look closely at that pin? She said yes Bec, hug therapist.... I said no Gam, the way it is set up... it says Hug the rapist! Well, I don't think I saw it on her after that day but... she was always the best hugger...

When I was 9 years old, I will never forget the day I was told that my grandfather had passed away. I was heartbroken; he was an amazing man! I remember my mom coming to take me to the post funeral gathering since I was so young I didn't attend the funeral. I remember very vividly walking into the house where my Gamma was sitting by the piano with a black hat that had a veil on it. She sat with tears rolling down her cheeks. She tried to muster every bit of strength to move forward with life, she was a pilar in our family and had just lost the love of her life and father to her children, and our grandfather; for the last 41 years she has waited to be reunited with her love and I'm sure he has been waiting to be reunited with her! As hard as it is for us to lose her here on earth, they are together again... I'm sure the dancing that they are now dancing as Gampa is singing some Fiddler on the roof...that my Gams love, is once again singing in her ear! If I were a rich man, doo bee diddle didle dum... yes Gampa ... you are a very rich man ... your love is by your side once again ...now She can sing along too ... and I'm positive she is dancing!

As I sat beside your bed early Monday morning, I put my hand under yours, you took my hand and held it tight, I didn't ever want to let go! As people were leaving that room, bending to kiss your head, I think I may have been a little selfish as I couldn't let go of the grip you had on my hand! You weren't talking at that point, but you spoke volumes with that moment in time! Grace, dignity, love and faith ... strength, hope and your never-ending feistiness! Thank you for always being you!

My Gamma, we will miss you always, you raised us right, you loved us hard, you nurtured us softly, you gave us all the tools life needs us to have. Faith, hope and love! The example you were to each and every one of us will pass down for years to come and the life you led and the legacy you left us will live on! I love you forever! Xoxo

Toppy

She was my best friend
I was her Becca
I was her granddaughter
She was my Gam
A special bond we always had
I'm guessing from the start
She always held my hand
She will always hold my heart
Every day, sometimes twice
We chatted on the phone
We talked about such crazy things I never felt alone!
From morning coffee, to buttered toast
From gum soup to lemon squares
From beautiful heart beautiful soul
But cobwebs for her hairs
Going for a hairdo she'd say
New perm, fluff up...gorgeous!
Then my mom would do her thing
Final touches
One by one
Glue on her new lashes
Hand under chin
Flirty look
Then out the door she dashes
Ceramics teacher
Golfing girl
Bowling
Dancing
Having so much fun

Always time for those she loves
From jeans and t shirts
Dresses and fancy gloves
Not a day goes by
That I don't miss her advice
That I don't miss her belly laugh
Her hugs, her smiles, her life
Beautiful lady inside and out most beautiful
Loved us all more than anything
Without any doubt—

Every Stuff

Some look at things and see useless trash
Others look and see treasure
Some have a knack for making things
Giving them hours of creative pleasure v
Some can take those same weird things
Set them up just so.
Decorating places with objects
Deemed as junk by another
But always turned into amazing
By my mother
It's crazy how a pile of stuff
That people throw away
Mom can create
And make someone's day
Just like when God sees a broken person
Living in sadness and strife
He can change the situation
And give them brand new life
When I asked my son what Mammy likes
His reply was every stuff
Just like Jesus, He loves the weak and the tough
When God handed out mothers, I think He loves me best
Because He gave one to me that is better than the rest!—

Maddy and Colby

Two little people changed my world,
two little faces, a boy and a girl
Being with them, my heart beams
Hugs, kisses
Giggles and smiles
New words learned
Excitement filled screams
Coloring, dancing, playing, and singing
Outside running around or on the swing-set swinging.
Imaginations blooming
Jumping around
Musical instruments
Making new sounds
Pretend food, what can we make
Coffee for Mimi
For Papa
Some cake
Playing with
play doh
Rolling it out
Time with them is the best
Without any doubt
Trips to the playground
Off to the zoo
Children's Museum
So much fun with both of you!
Splashing in the water
Playing in the sand
Walking to the front door

We all hold hands
Reading you stories
Watching you grow
Is my greatest blessing
I want you to know!—

Dear Somebody,

There are many places and areas
I think you need to grow
If you look deep within
I think you already know
Immaturity and irresponsibility
Looks like lack of ability
Constant exhaustion or lack of sleep
It is part of being a grown-up and a parent
Talk is cheap
Hearing the truth is really tough
Feeling less than is really rough
Getting what you know you need
stepping up and taking heed
No more playing silly games
Calling out the issues
Naming them by names
No more excuses
No more lies
No more tears and no more cries
No more stories
No more insult
It's time to grow up and be an adult!—

Music Man

Tapping of your fingers
Making beats with your hands
Creating music
Repetitive noise
Like a genuine one-man band
Little did I know
The songs that you tapped
Was your magnificent brain releasing
An artist inside that was trapped
Marching to your own drum
To find out who you are
Stepping to your own song
Taking you so far
Next, there was the piano
Fingers roll across the keys
Then Ukulele strumming
Finding notes we could not see
One man band
Writing text
Composing songs
What could be next
Take your talent to the stage
Exposing deepest fears
Igniting emotions
Both sad and happy tears
One man band
Always reaching
For a brand-new beat
Sharing from the heart

Taking music to the street
Music man
Gifted
Expressive chorus
Burden lifted
Sharing dreams
Sometimes hiding
Behind a mask of outward peace
But inside
Composing always
As a way of sweet release—

Popcorn Nose

Broken little girl
Scared little heart
Trauma piercing right from the start
Scared and alone
So hungry so small
Wrapped in a small blanket
By the angry waterfall
I'm only an infant
Why am I here
Can somebody help
I'm crying in fear
Then some man I did not know
Heard my loud cries from the street
He ran down the hill to find me
Screaming and kicking my feet.
Now what will happen
Where will I go
My face is all over
Every single news show.
They took me to the hospital to make sure I'm ok
Then found me a family for my temporary stay.
Finally safe and finally fed,
Why does the social system think it's ok
They send me back and forth to visit the unknown
Unsafe situations, my stomach felt like stone.
Trauma repeated trauma almost enforced
Seemingly social services don't care if I get lost.
Sending me back

Making me stay
So, trauma can repeat every day.
Where are my people
5 years have gone by
Does social services know
All I do is cry
Trauma again
Oh, wait is that my dad
He found me here
Maybe now I won't have to be sad
Slowly and gently, he made his way in
Then trauma was just a little less
As I visited my real home again.
My mommy is ecstatic
My siblings are so kind
But all I could do was worry about who I left behind
One sister, one brother who needed me there
They are still stuck in the trauma
By still being there!
I went back and forth
I did my best
Until that one day I could kind of rest.
Social services realized they made a big mistake
My sister and brother, they also would take.
Trauma still rages
Trauma steals so much
Trauma takes away my faith and my trust
Also makes Healing so hard to touch.
More trauma has hit me
Some cause even worse distress,
Trauma to add to the pile of my life
Feeling quite buried in mess

It's time to let God one step at a time
Begin to Heal each big gaping hole
It's time to let your guard down
Let healing begin
Finally get some peace for your soul!—

My Emily

I could not be prouder
Of the woman that you are
The journey has been hard sometimes
But you have come so far
Looking back at the footprints
Made on your path
Handprints on your bedroom wall
Struggling with math
Three big brothers
One your very best friend
The other two drove you nuts
Will that ever end?
Watching you grow
Challenges you face
Health issues, depression, anxiety
Yet you handle it all with grace
I couldn't be more thankful
That I get to be your mom
I wish there was a way for me to
To calm every storm
You
My girl
Are amazing
You
My girl
are smart
You
My girl
Beautiful

You Are my world
And my whole heart
Every step you take
Move with your head held high
Every step you take
Know you are loved past the moon and sky
I believe in you
Even when you doubt
I believe in you
Through every tear
I believe in you
With every step you take
I believe in you
Every victory, every fear
Embrace the day
One second at a time
Even when you're down
Remember who you are
Then....
Straighten that crown!
I love you so much!
Sorry if I'm a sap
This is what I do
At night when I should be sleeping
All I do is nap!!! —

Hey Mr. PJ

Three days of labor
Eight-and-a-half-pound baby boy
My fifth child
Filled my life with joy
Growing up is not always easy
Being the baby of the pack
Three big brothers and a sister
Attention never at a lack
Five years later you became
A big brother
You were so gentle
So sweet
Like no other
Watching you grow
From a boy to a man
So much has happened in your life span
Trauma hit you hard at a very young age
Something you had to handle
Could have filled you with rage
Instead, my boy, you did not do that
Your sweet sensitive heart
Tried to move forward with life
Love our times of general chat
I'm so proud to be your mom
You do your best everyday
Your hardworking, kind, and giving
Keep striving for your best
Try to not just live to work but work to make life worth living

Kindness
Love
Genuine guy
Helpful and giving Keep striving
You make a mama proud! —

Father's Day

Dear David,
Sometimes Fathers are not who we think
Sometimes they may not have biological kids
Though they dreamed of it all of their lives
But God in His choosing
Made you be a dad
to countless little people
With no good man in their life to be had!
The influence of wisdom
The blessing of Grace
The heart of love
Written over your face
The gift of a hug
Sometimes a tear to share
The listening ear
Your willingness to share
Sometimes belly laughs
Sometimes serious talk
Speak volumes to many
Of with whom, you walk
You radiate Jesus
You share so much
Your words of encouragement
There are so many you touch
While Gods plan isn't seen yet
Your heart may not know
But the Lord Himself
Has you helping so many to grow.

While it may not be the fatherhood
You may have had in mind
I know that to many
You are one of a kind
So, know you are loved
By so many
Happy Father's Day
My friend —

To My Therapist

Open my mind
Share my heart
Talking about life and things from the start
Gently and calmly
Open and kind
Comforting wisdom
Clearing my mind
No judgement of fears
Emptying and processing
The trauma I have had buried for so many years
Safe place
Caring soul
Dedicating her life to helping people be whole
Appropriately named
God knew she had a gift
Even when things are really heavy
Somehow the heavy lifts
If you take the word caring
The first letters are in her name, Cari
Healing hearts, healing shame
Talking through hurt
Processing grief
Offering kindly, The way to relief—

Bridges

Things most take for granted
Ofttimes it isn't thought about
Going to some places can be difficult
There isn't any doubt
Access for everyone to places we go
Are not usually accessible
People need to know
Going to the beach, navigation of the land
Trying to make the way to the water
Can we make it through the sand?
Going to a restaurant
A flight of stairs is what I see
My family can go in and eat
But I cannot climb up that flight
This place is not for me.
Taking things, we all do everyday
Not thinking about navigation
For some, there are several words to consider
Accessibility, safety, what if there is a need for evacuation?
Is there a safe way in?
Is there a safe way out?
Everywhere has potential to be available
It needs to be figured out
Hearing a phrase from a friend today
I may not be able to stand up, but I can stand out
Advocating for inclusive accessibility
Is what it's all about!
Going on a sailboat
Specially designed for all to ride

Wheelchairs access freely
Enjoy the water, wind and the fresh air, just being outside
Experiencing adventure
Taking trips
Knowing there is accessibility is key
Making memories
Happy ones
For my family, friends and me!—

3

Mama's Heart

MAMA'S HEART

Mama's heart never stops Loving
Mama's heart never stops Worrying
Mama's heart never stops Praying
Mama's heart never Gives up
Mama's heart Gets worried
Mama's heart Gets scared
Mama's heart Gets broken
Mama's heart Gets weary
Mamas' eyes get Red
Mama's eyes get Teary
Mama's eyes get Scared
Mama's eyes get sad
From the minute you were conceived
That second, I believed that there was nothing in this world that I would not do to make sure you are okay.
I don't care if you're 1 or 100 I'm there by your side. Throughout this ride called life.
It gets hard, Things get hard
You get yourself into things and don't think you can get out. Don't let those things rob you of who you know you are!
Who I know you are.
I will fight for you
I will fight with you
I will fight you!
But I will NEVER EVER QUIT making sure you are okay!
I love you with my soul, you're part of me and always will be.
Love, Mama—

Hair

Gray hairs multiply on my head
Able bodied people
hang out in their bed.

I carry bags up.
I cook the food.
Even though I'm really not in the mood.

Then the dishes
Stacked up high.
Seems like nobody else sees them.
my oh my

Walking in the house to random junk here and there
Adding yet another one to my head of gray hair
Climb the stairs and look around.
Oh, look someone left dirty socks right there on the ground.

Walk a little further into another space.
Table with boxes of takeout,
crumbs and more trash
I Try to show grace.

Over to the right where dishes fill the sink.
Dishwasher only a bend away
But it's ok, just leave them there to stink.

Fruit flies multiply every day.
Does anyone notice?
Or is it just more for me to say?

Once again, I clean up only to make another big mess.
Only to produce more gray hair and cause me so much stress.
How can I make it clear to all who are around?
Do I whisper? Should I scream?
Do silent tears make a sound?

Why are you lazy? Am I simply crazy?
Is it too much to ask for you to take care of your own crap?
To wake up and look around, stop taking a nap.

Life passes by
Relaxing is rare.
All I seem to get around here is more and more gray hair!—

Depression

The feeling is empty
The feeling is real
The world just keeps spinning around
The heavy I feel
deep down in my soul
The weight on my shoulders
Keeps Holding me down
I raise my arms
I fall to the ground
What must I do
To free my heart from this ache
I must take a step forward
Take another one too
Remember I AM NOT A MISTAKE!
My life has a purpose
But what could it be
How can I step forward with this gripping me
Take a deep breath
Hold it for five
Then blow the air out
Start feeling alive
Let's do it again and count back from 10
Nine, eight, seven, six, five
Start feeling alive
Keep counting back down
Let it calm all your fears
When you finish this. exhale
Then wipe off the tears
Inhale slowly again

Close your eyes and feel peace
Remember
I matter
To myself
To my family and friends
Another step forward
Remember to breathe deeply
Let peace cover your heart
When you open your eyes
Take another step forward
I'm ready for a new start—

Fried

How many balls can one person juggle
How can you sit there and watch me struggle
I wake up every morning to start another day
Still half out of it and stressed
Walk over to my closet to look for a shirt
Paint my smile on my face and get dressed
Drive here, drive there get the kids make dinner
I want to pull out my hair
There are no words to explain the frustration I feel
When able bodied people
Sit and wait for their meal
I don't like this, one says
What's in this and why
Do I have to eat this?
 followed by whines
I am so frustrated that I want to explode
My painted smile covers my anger untold
Don't worry everybody
 Stay in your chair
You're going to find out soon I'm not there
To wait on you with both my hands and my feet
You will find out what it's like to be back on the street
The free ride is over
Can't do this no more
Why can't you pick up a broom and sweep the damn floor
Oh, wait no worries
I will get that too
Just leave the crap everywhere
I'll tell you to screw!—

Struggles

Sometimes life throws you curve ball after curve ball and sometimes you get hit by the ball and other times, we learn to dodge them or catch them and take control of them! Most of my life I have struggled with so many giant obstacles and people will say they just don't know How I do it! Well to be honest I move one day at a time and sometimes a minute at a time! A few years ago, I decided to take control of one of my largest battles and was conquering successfully, I was getting healthy, confident and moving myself into a new "me", Then when my world exploded and life took me on a new journey, I found my struggle to be harder than ever to conquer. I gained back all the weight I lost, I quit the gym, I ate junk, I gave up on myself again. I got submerged in the chaos life has given me! I have used excuses that I have too much to do, and I have no time... to maybe tomorrow... I have scheduled time slots for myself to go in my planner but always seemed to find other unavoidable things to fill my time! Truth be told I was afraid to start and afraid to get control of me again... afraid that my world would shatter again, afraid to let anyone tell me otherwise. Afraid to let anyone really love me and afraid to let myself be ok! As I write this my sneakers are laced up for the first time in a few years... my heart is in this, and my mind is ready! I am taking ME back!

Coping Skills

Sometimes exhausted does not quite say
Sometimes it's the wrong word
When life seemingly throws things at us
From every single way
Take a deep breath
Then close my eyes
Trying to focus on the beat within my chest
Breathe in through my nose 1..2..3..4
Out through my mouth 1..2..3..4
Repeat as many times as you need
Until you feel some rest.—

Dear Mama

Dear Mama,

You don't need to take care of everything all the time, you don't have to be the best mom, the best housewife, or superwoman.

Sometimes when your body gets tired, there will be few who will remember that you tried to be all of this all by yourself and you didn't have to.

So, leave the cleaning for later, go for a drive, go to the park, buy clothes, take a walk, go to the salon, take a nap, be yourself, take care of yourself, love yourself, and do it. JUST FOR YOU!

We will grow up, have a family of our own, but you can't be replaced! The house will get dirty again, but you don't get a second chance at living life to the fullest!

Love,
the Kids.

Where?

Sometimes I feel myself falling down a hole
Can't seem to climb my way out
Every day I wake up
There are so many more things
That I find to stress myself about
The trials keep piling
My mind overwhelmed
I'm no longer smiling
Feeling so tired and all alone
In a room full of people, I feel like a stone
Hard on the outside it goes pretty deep, tears built up on the inside, it is so hard to sleep.
The pressure I put on myself is sometimes too much.
Trying to learn to say no
Yet every day more things are asked of me
I am constantly on the go.
Sitting now in this quiet room
Thinking of things that I need to get done.
But there is nothing I can think of that I want to do
I can't seem to find anything fun.
What is wrong with me
Why am I so down
Why is my face always in a frown
Why does it seem like I'm pushing away
Falling down the hole again
Is this where I stay?—

Oz

Head to the plow
No looking back
So many hurdles
Overwhelming stack
Head to the plow
The future uncertain
Wizard of oz
Man behind curtain
Feeling alone
I just want to go free
Tap my heels together
One two three
Open my eyes
Pushing the plow
Eyes looking forward
Eye on the prize
Feeling like tin man
My muscles are tight
Don't know the last time
I slept through the night
Feeling like scarecrow
Where is my brain
So many things to do, am I going insane?
Feeling like lion
Looking for courage
It's there just receive it
Don't be discouraged
Feel like the munchkins
Running scattered and scared

Rebecca Almeida

Then I remember who numbered my hairs
God feels like Auntie Em
Calling my name
Waiting so patiently
For me to let Him win the game
Feeling like toto
Need to follow the road
God has set before me
Wants to lighten my load.
Feeling like Dorothy
Just want to go home
God says He never left
He has been there all along
Take heart in knowing
That no matter what
God has you in His Hand
Living in your heart—

Wishes

Every day I wish we could
Do the things that other families would
A ride to the zoo, outside to play ball
A play date, the library, even the mall
Planning a party each year on your day
Trying and hoping somehow, someway
Wish you could Enjoy just a day just as you are
Instead, you're trapped in your own head,
We cannot go far
What's happening
What's got you
How can we get in?
These times we can't get through to you
I don't know where to begin
Can you hear us?
Can you see?
It just doesn't seem like you're listening to me
You're screaming but we don't know why
Your confusion, your anger, your cry
I wish we could, it makes me sad
When I think of the fun that could be had
You're missing out and so are we
We are stuck in this merry go round
We cannot see
We keep hoping that something will help
To ease the struggle inside
We keep on trying, but we can't seem to help
What can we do to get you off of this ride?

Artist is Janiah, age 9

Artist is Shiloh, age 8

Life

There are days I get all of my best thinking and ideas as I drive from appointment to appointment wondering how I am going to get done all I have to do. My mind races, my brain spends a lot of time on overload. I can't physically juggle but find myself juggling more tasks than I thought possible.

People have asked me how I do it. How do I manage with all life has given me at any given moment. My experience ranges from being the oldest child in a house full of biological, adopted and foster siblings. Every day coming home not knowing who was going to be around the kitchen table for dinner. Being a sister, a friend, a babysitter, diaper changer, bath giver, booboo kisser, food maker, drink getting, teenager. Life was busy!

Now as an adult with kids of my own, all with some challenge or another, I have found that somedays I am on autopilot. I wake up and just walk around doing things like a robot. I wonder a lot where am I in all of this crazy? Have I lost myself and my ability to be me? How do I find time to debrief from the nonsense that is life? I also had undiagnosed ADHD, so I have a trail of me wherever I go. Unfinished projects, laundry to fold, papers to file, refrigerator to clean, grocery shopping to do, and the list goes on and on.

I have found that stopping for a minute most days doesn't really happen for me. My mind goes nonstop, and I can't seem to relax. SO, if you feel this, you're not alone. We as parents all juggle and feel like we are forgetting something. As a special needs mama, it plays games with your mind because not only do you have to do your job, but you have to also do other people's jobs as well. Chasing services to ensure your child has whatever they need. Let's face it, life is tough, but if you put yourself in Gods Hands and let Him handle it, (I keep trying to help Him and take stuff back) it will be much easier to do. So, take a deep breath and give yourself some grace. You're doing a great job, even when you don't see it for yourself! Taking space to breathe even if just for a minute is OK and encouraged. YOU are the only YOU there is. SO, as the saying goes, "Put on your own oxygen mask first!" Be well!

Phases

Ofttimes, I overcompensate
Buy things I think you might enjoy
I step in where I see a need
More times I just annoy
My heart is sad
I will try to help
As of now I must step back
Thinking about the whys last night
There are things I can't take back
First was your father
He left a huge hole in your heart
By being irresponsible and abusive from the start
Then the times I had checked out
Lost my brain is what it seemed
This wasn't what I wanted for us
Not even close to what I dreamed
Then along came the next one even meaner than the first
All I saw was he paid his bills
Not the alcohol that quenched his thirst
I didn't know he was abusive
I didn't know he broke your soul
I didn't know that was happening
I was Trauma reactive living in my own hole
Here I am all these years later
Unconsciously trying to fix what's wrong
Stepping in to take care of things
Stepping in where I don't belong
We all have serious trauma
Some are working on it

Some are not
My heart is just so broken
I wish I could give you all a new start
For now, the best I can do
Is take a giant step back
Give you all your own space
Just fill in if I see dangerous lack!
I love all endlessly
To be corny, to the moon and back!—

SAD TRUTH

Sitting
Silent
Tears rolling
Eyes burn
Feel alone
Just because
I'm home
Doesn't mean
I'm bored
Overwhelmed
So much to do
Pile more
And more
And more
Why
Idk
I just don't know—

Sticky Note

Fighting battles that keep seeming to win
Grief PTSD and sadness
In your head constantly spin
Distant thoughts from every place
Horrible memories
Can't seem to erase
Reaching for things to numb the deep pain
Trying so hard to resist
Running from help
But saying you're not
Lying to those trying to assist
Fear in your eyes
Emptiness in your smile
Sadness in your heart
A glimmer of hope once in a while
Steps you must take whether you like it or not
Steps that are so hard
Steps to start healing your heart
So many losses
So much pain
But stop, look and listen to the blessings that you gain
Close your eyes
Take a deep breath
Count your blessings one at a time
Release the sad with each deep exhale
Let one thing out then the next
Take another fresh breath
Take in some more good stuff, counting blessings one by one

Thank God for another day to begin again
With happy thoughts in your mind

When you get a thought... a good one write it on a sticky note and stick it where you can see it often
When you get sad thoughts Write it down on a different sticky note ... take a minute with it, then rip it up and put it in the trash!
Don't let it ruin you today —

Reflections

When I look into a mirror
The person that I see
Is someone I don't recognize
But that person is me
On the outside things look ok
The smile to hide the pain
But the inside feels weathered
Like thunderstorms and rain
Thoughts race like the tide
Crashing to and fro
Trying to find calm
A Quiet, peaceful place to go
My body feels restless
my heart
Pounding fast
A still small voice inside my heart
Whispers to me at last
Close my eyes
Take a minute
What did the small voice say
Trust me with your insecurities
It will all be okay
Open my eyes
Then I Look again
At the reflection of my face
Hold onto the hope in your soul
Walk forward with faith and grace!—

Artist is Lucy, age 15

I Don't Even Know

Not suicidal
Don't want to die
Look around
Just want to cry
violence, hate
Sadness, stress
Senseless, depression
People irate
Can't read the headlines
Can't turn on the news
Its killing, stabbing,
Wars, and rape
Instilling fear
From the evil it spews
God, please help us
Protect our minds
Take the fear
Heal the anxiety
The paralyzing kind
Trying to trust
Giving all to You
Trying not to hold onto rage
The poison of evil
It is soaking up fast
Putting young people in a spiritual cage
Believing lies
that looks to be truth
Fighting things, they have deep in their heart
God please, give them a nudge
Remind them what they learned from the start!—

Broken Me

Room full of people around
Talking and laughing so loud
Yet I feel so isolated
Can't relate to the sound.
It's all so loud
At the same time, it's not
So many feelings are going on in my heart
How can I tell you what's going on
How can I pinpoint
Where do I start
Is it the children who struggle every day
Is it pressure I put on myself
To fix things my way.
Is it being on call to go here and there
Or the handling problems
feels Like everywhere
Is it worry, fear, or the weary eyes
Is it anger, frustration or the hours my heart cries
Is it failure as a mom?
Did I do something bad
Is it something I did
That makes them so sad.
I have spent my life trying to make it ok
And fight, advocate, try to have a say

I feel like I'm in a big losing battle
Like riding a horse and falling off of the saddle
Holding on to the reigns
Holding on for dear life

Hoping to make it through
Endless days of strife
I'm tired,
I'm sad,
I'm trying to be alright
Really, I am.
But stuff just keeps
Piling with no end in sight
If you see me
And my load looks heavy
Please take a bag even if I resist
I'm stubborn, you know ... you may have to insist—

Endless

So many things I regret
So many things I can't change
So many things make me angry
So many things are strange
So many things make me cry
So many things make me sad
So many things make me want to run
So many things make me so mad
So many times, I can't seem to breathe
So many times, the frustration makes me feel sick
So many times, I want to just leave
Sometimes I despise being a mom
Sometimes I crave peace and quiet
Sometimes I want to just be alone
Sometimes I feel stuck in this riot
So many things so many times
No seeming reasons for their melt downs
Nothing makes sense
I feel so disconnected from all the things I love
But the question is this .... Do I or am I stuck in a rollercoaster or madness causing me so much sadness?—

WAVES

Have you ever gone to the beach
Then run into the water
Excited for the first big wave to come
Looking and waiting in wonder
The wave approaches, it hits you hard
It drops you on your face
You skin your knee on a rock
A wound that won't erase
Wiping the water from your eyes
You stand back up when you are able
Bury your feet in the sand
Trying to make sure you're standing stable
Waiting there for a minute
For another wave to land
You're going to try to beat the hit
Firm and steady you attempt to stand
But the force it knocks you down
Just be still, just sit
Struggling to stand back up again
The sand beneath you scatters
I look at the next wave in the face
Getting back up is all that matters
Here comes another giant wave
This one's not going to get me
Only to go down again, and wound the other knee
Dust yourself off,
from the muck and the mud
Then stand up for another
Hoping this time that you can stay up

That you will feel no thud
Filled with excitement, anticipation and more
When the big wave approaches
You fall to the floor.
This time you get up with a look in your eye
You stare the big wave down.
How many times will you battle these waves
You feel yourself starting to frown.
You look at the water
Feeling defeat
here comes yet another big test
But it crashes to the ground
Hitting the sand
Before it reaches your feet.
You're standing and looking in awe
As the water gets still
You take a deep breath
take in the peace
Gather your strength
Inhale
Then exhale
Let all the fear be released
Don't be afraid to fall in the water
It will always clear
Always stand right back up,
So, you can finally let go of the fear
Take time to reflect on the day
Then look right at the waves with confidence
knowing
I will make it through all of this someday!—

Dedicated to my dad, Bill

Artist is Izzy, age 10

House divided

Every decision every day
Someone gets upset somehow
Some way
Why is he here
He doesn't deserve a chance
I'm not speaking to him
He gave me a nasty glance
It's very difficult to live with him I know
The choices are so limited
No places he can go
Tears that break my heart
Keep rolling down my face anger hurt and destruction
Things he did, I can't erase
Then the anger felt
Toward people in my life
The silence from the others
Causes so much strife
They are unaware of the anger that is raging
They go on about their lives
Thinking all is well
because they are engaging
The outward attempt at helping sometimes feels like forced bonding
The inward attempts at seeking the help needed
Seemingly not responding
The lies, excuses, the sneaking just hurts
I'm tired of watching the responsibility of what's happening get shirked.
When others look into the children's eyes and see the damage done
Then think about their brother and how he has been my absent son.
Some don't want to be around; some people are here.

The anger that is raging from all the others
Just won't disappear
Does anyone realize the effects on sisters and brothers?
Here I sit tears in my eyes
Trying to make sense
Of all of the lies
Here I sit, tightness in my chest
The stress of it all
Can't get any rest
Here I sit knots in my back
The tension all around me
Can't get this on track
Truth, I am angry
Truth I am sad
Truth I am afraid
It all makes me so mad
Truth I am terrified
Truth I am tired of lies
Truth, I want some peace from it all
Don't want sad tears in my eyes
Reality is hard
Life is tough
Sometimes what you think is right
Just isn't enough
Some sacrifices you just have to take
Some hard choices you just have to make
Boundaries
Respect
Putting your feelings aside
Stopping the insanity
Stopping this horrible ride
Take a look inside your heart
What is the best

Not just for yourself
But all of the rest
Innocent lives
Lives all unsure
By adults who made bad decisions
I'm watching these kids grow
From the biggest to the smallest
One, a victim of mental health wreck
The triplets, omg the mess what the heck
Now we are working to keep side effects at bay
The consequences of addiction
They horror they can all face
The division it's all caused between all of the grown
It makes my heart question
Why? am I wrong?
Should I give up? Or do I still fight?
Do I make sure every single one of them gets what is right?
Yes!!! —

Glimpses

When people see the outside
But they don't understand
That all the weight you carry
It is a representation of the pain your heart holds
People don't realize that ridicule and jokes don't help, only further the pain
Only deepen our own self disdain
Every jab or secret remark
Is another pound holding us down
On our journey we embark
Does anyone understand?
Seatbelt extender's
Chairs with arms
Booths in a restaurant are so tight
Amusement park rides, just cannot fit
Shopping for clothes and settling
Not because it's cute
but it fits
It's all part of the fight
Dieting is hard
Nothing seems to work
Restrictions again feel like you're out of place.
Constant self judgement
constant self-hate
Trying to pretend that you're fine.
What we all really need is support and acceptance in the end
Instead of making jokes
Try being a friend!—

Beautiful Chaos

So here is a little glimpse into the beautiful chaos called my life.

Life has a way of changing, and learning to ride the waves and climb up from deep valleys can feel like such a challenge sometimes. I found when I turn around to see where I came from and where I stand today, my steps are ordered. They feel like they are running in circles sometimes forward, sometimes backward, sometimes it honestly feels like I'm in a high-speed blender!!!

The kids are good; my older ones amaze me with the fantastic humans they have become.

The littles struggle day by day for every little milestone taken for granted, Mental Illness is a raging beast... it hurts, it exhausts, it divides... services to help are inadequate. Clinicians are tired. Families... well life is very different when you have a child with behavioral health and mental health issues... avoiding birthday parties, trips to the park or zoo... family gatherings... to say it is challenging doesn't really do it justice. Losing friends, on and on.... but we fight this battle every day! Through the challenges, I have developed friendships with people who are fierce like me!

Life has a funny way of changing! I love some of the changes, and I am embracing them as best I can! Others are extremely difficult and somedays I have to drop my gloves and cry. Some days I have to take a break from the fight because of the pressure it puts on my own mental health. But I will never give up this battle. Our children are worth every battle scar we have.

Much love to all!! Xoxo

4

Children's Mental Health

Words

Words cut deep.
You cannot take them back.
Words do things to your heart.
Healing is hard.
Forgiveness is needed.
Now to figure out where we start
Disrespectful behavior
Yelling, being rude.
Talking to your parents with such a nasty attitude
Somewhere inside, when you are acting like that.
Somewhere inside, not this nasty brat.
You do things, you spew hate, where does it come from?
Why do you want to hurt?
the ones who love you most?
I just do not understand!
Why do you say such hateful things?
Take a look inside yourself.
What is going on?
Why is nothing ever your fault?
Look inside!
Look at yourself and stop blaming others!—

Middle of the Night Thoughts

So many topics rush through my mind.
Running around everyday
So many projects, so many demands
Some days I just want to run away.
Waking up to demands from my 10-year-old son.
Wanting all kinds of things
If his needs are not met immediately
A major tantrum is what he will bring.
Starting my day like this makes me so tired.
Feeling so weary and drained
The mental health issues take over his mind.
His eyes glaze over.
The violence begins.
Then watching my son get restrained.
Why does this happen?
Why is this so hard?
Why can't he just calm himself down?
Take some deep breaths.
Sometimes it takes hours to rest.
His staff is by his side.
Always giving their best.
How can we reach you in these distant times?
How can we help you?
What do you need?
There are no reasons, no rhymes.
I am just exhausted; my mind will not slow down.
So here I sit in the middle of the night.
Thinking and mulling around
We all try to help you.

While hearing your cries
What could you be thinking?
behind those confused eyes
There is nothing I want more than to help calm you down.
Help change your little heart to a smile.
Not a frown
So many topics run through my head.
Trying to figure what makes you see red.
It must be so scary when your brain gets so stuck.
Hoping each time, it happens
We have some good luck.
Please know when you are broken and losing control
I love you always from the depths of my soul!—

Everyday RAD

Every day my heart gets broken.
Every day hateful words are spoken.
Every day selfish child
Disrespectful
Disappointed
Disobedience...
WILD
What to do
Do I keep trying?
What to do
With constant lying
Speaking words of utter dislike
I cannot say a word.
I cannot do anything right.
on the verge
Of giving up on this fight
The constant need to hurt and put down.
To call me stupid
My heart in constant frown
I am tired of being abused.
I am tired of the hurt.
I am tired of crying.
You are treating me like dirt.
I am sorry.
I am not rude.
I am not disrespectful.
I do not give attitude.
These are all the things I hear each and every day.
All of the words you constantly say.

No longer have meaning.
They bounce off the wall.
Feeling the pain of the abuse
It makes my skin crawl.
What should I do?
Should I just walk away? The reality of that statement....
getting close every day!!!—

The Boy Inside

Reading you a story
Then turn down the light.
Kiss you on your forehead.
Then we say good night
But wait mommy there are things you really need to know.
One is that I love you.
Two is that need you.
Three is that you love me.
Four you need me too.
I may be hard to understand.
It may be tough to see.
When my temper tantrums
Start taking over me.
I say mean things.
I hit your face.
I spit, kick, and bang my head.
I say that I hate this place.
I want to say just one more thing.
It's coming from my heart.
When I say the things, I say to you.
And my temper is off the chart.
Please mommy, know I really love you.
I do not mean the things I say.
I want to be the boy inside.
Each and every day
The boy inside is loving.
The boy inside is kind.
The boy inside is funny.
The boy inside my mind

Wants you to know.
That I love you.
Though Sometimes it does not show.
But mommy in those moments
When hurt covers your entire soul.
Remember me the boy inside,
Just want to be whole!—

Sweet Boy

The overwhelming guilt
Can't see through the tears.
Decisions are so hard.
There are so many fears.
Looking at you and how you have grown through the years.
The struggles you have faced.
The trauma endured.
When I look in your eyes my sweet child
The love in my heart explodes.
The pain in your eyes
The broken parts in your brain
Caused by the neglect of a mother in pain.
How can we help you?
What can we do?
The smile inside
You shine like the sun.
But the broken parts the challenges face
seem to overcome.
I will not give up on you.
The trial will not win.
I promised when I met you.
Our bond to begin.
I cannot imagine what it's like
To live with all the noise
The struggle in your brain consumes.
Trying to destroy
But my dear I will not Quit.
My heart you have forever
I will fight for your mental health.
Will I give up? NEVER!—

Another

Another call to 911
Another outburst has begun.
Another time you smash your head,
Another time locked in your bed.
Another fist you hit your face.
Another scar we cannot erase.
Another bad name you do not mean.
Another bite mark another scream.
Another police car is coming here.
Another ambulance to take you there.
Another time you beg to stay.
Another time we try to delay.
Another broken heart I feel.
Another day this is surreal.
Another ride to the emergency room
Another doctor
Another night in gloom
Another round of tears that fall.
Another hole made in the wall.
Another night of broken sleep
Another and another, how much more
Another still
Another door
Another phone call
Another plea
Another Please mommy, can you help me?—

Do You?

Do you have any idea?
What it is like to be us
To wake up every morning
To some kind of fuss

Before my eyes even open
Before the coffee gets brewed
I am yelled at and screamed at
It is really quite rude.

Within minutes it starts the bag drops in the floor
Theres a trail of poop coming from her door.
The next one gets up screaming, mom she is gross.
Then they want to have breakfast.
They only want toast.

Then changing the bag just like last night
Only this time she puts up one hell of a fight.
It takes a long time to get her cleaned up, dressed and fed.
Another morning of crazy every morning I dread.

Stand still, please stop moving.
I am sorry it hurts.
But we have to get it done.
Every morning with chaos
It is really no fun!—

RAD

Words
Cut like daggers.
Ripping my soul
Hate spewing easily.
So much anger takes a toll.
I love you,
I hate you.
I'm sorry.
Are you mad?
No, not really but my heart feels so incredibly sad!
Trying to understand
It breaks me down a little further each time.—

Thumbs

I sit here watching.
I sit here waiting.
They came down to ask about you and what brings us here again.
We go through your history.
I will tell them once more.
About how you struggle then throw yourself on the floor.
Frustrated and angry, nobody knows why.
Biting and hitting, grabbing your bag
We have no idea what makes you cry.
Is something hurting?
Do you even know?
While you sit there sucking your thumb
What could it be going on in your head?
Where can we get some answers from!
From the moment our eyes met when you were so small
Your thumb was your comfort we know.
Now here we sit almost twelve years later.
That thumb in your mouth wherever you go.—

Dear K,

Awake most of the night.
Are we doing the right thing?
Worrying about what's happening.
What does the future bring?
Trying and trying to keep you safe here at home
So lost in your own head.
Where'd my little girl go?
One minute you are silent.
The next chronic aggression
The next laughing hysterically
So sad to watch so much regression.
Hitting and making threats
Wanting everyone to die
So far gone.
You cannot even cry
Rocking, demanding, asking for things that do not exist.
Finally settling, not really calming, still the constant resist
Thumb in your mouth
Blank look on your face
Staring at nothing
Your brain is stuck in this place.
Missing your giggles, the ones that aren't manic.
Missing your sassiness when it was not filled with panic.
Missing you being you
Silly and sweet
Dancing and singing
Clumsy on your feet
Seems like all the days filled with breath holding and fear.
Can't seem to fix this year after year.

Facing decisions with steps we must take.
Decisions so gut wrenching
But there are ones we must make.
Keeping you safe and watching you grow
Are things that my heart wants more than you know.
Lying awake for most of the night
My baby girl
She is out of my sight.
Wondering if she thinks her mommy walked away.
But my little girl at the end of every day
I cry myself to sleep.
Thinking of a way, dreaming of a day
That you and your brothers can be free from the mess.
That goes on inside your head.
Free from
Mental illnesses cause such distress.
In the meantime, mommy fights
Trying to get you the best of what you need
Even if it means continued sleepless nights!
I love you K—

But are you?

Helpful and sweet
One flip of a switch and it is nasty you meet.
Where does the nice you go?
Why do you hide?
Why are you so selfish and mean?
Seemingly, so full of pride
Masking the trauma
Hiding the pain
Making sure loud thunder
Comes with lightning and rain.
I am sorry is said
Wait.
Here it comes on repeat.
Demanding
Obnoxiously
Stomping your feet
I am tired of fighting.
I am tired of stress.
I do not believe your I'm sorry.
Causing so much distress
But I love you.
But do you?
Yes, Mommy, I do.
I love you Mommy.
Mommy does not think it's true.
Mommy is hurt.
Mommy is sad.
Mommy is tired.
Mommy is mad.

Mommy is distant.
Mommy shuts the door.
Because every day
Mommy's heart breaks
just a little bit more—

Artist is Adrianna, age 10

Storms

Raining emotions
Thunderstorms brew.
Lightning strikes
What can we do?
Snowing tears
Frozen heart
Closing off
Try not to feel.
Another day about to start.
 Sleet of feeling
A mixture of mess
Overwhelmed
Exhausted
Everywhere I look.
Stress
Hail is falling.
Big chunks of ice
Naming each piece
With the traumas
Not nice
Abuse, neglect, severe depression!
Autism, delays
So much aggression
Self-absorbed people
All kinds of addiction
Mental health issues
This must be a joke…
Is this life fake or is it nonfiction?—

Triplets

October 16, 2011
I got a gift sent straight from heaven.
One two and three sent straight to me.
Each one is different but special you see.
Somedays we have our challenges.
Sometimes things are tough.
but we stick together even though it can get rough.
I promised you then.
I promise you today.
I will stick with you every step of the way.
when you feel tired and when you feel sad,
I know sometimes it feels like you just get really mad.
I know it's really hard to be where you are.
but in my heart, you are never that far.
I love you every single day,
more than I can ever say.
The struggles you face day in and day out.
We all try to understand what it is all about
We try to talk.
We will try to help.
We try everything we know.
And nothing....
What do you need?
Please tell me.
How can I reach you?
What can I do?
What am I missing?
Somewhere, in there are my sweet little ones.
Who fill my heart and outshine the sun

The sparkle in your eyes, the smiles on your faces
The laughter from your bellies
No one can erase.
Hugs, love, the genuine child
Buried beneath this mess.
How can we unmask my sweet little ones?
Living in constant distress
I cannot wait till you are home every day. Keep working hard, I will keep doing what I am doing, being behind you, cheering you on, praying for the day that you can all be OK.
Love, Mommy—

Childhood Inpatient

Brand new bikes
Toys still in the box
New clothes with tags
Keep the underwear and socks.
Pants have strings.
Sweatshirts have hoods.
Can't have those either.
Understood
At birthday time, only two can come.
You cannot bring your phone.
Can't facetime and share with everyone.
Disconnected
Is a word used for unhooking plugs?
For kids in psychiatric hospitals
We get pumped with more drugs.
One for anxiety
One for aggression
One for ADHD
One for depression
Somewhere
My child is in there.
Trying to regulate
From chaos and despair
Missing out on childhood
Can't seem to find their feet.
Spending lots of time
Sitting in a seat
Should not know what rounds are.
Should know what it's like to play.

Should not be needing a PRN.
Each and every day.
Shouldn't sleep in a strange bed.
Without my family around
I should be resting in my own house.
My body safe and sound
Needing lots of love and support
Can't do things all alone.
But services that should be there
Can't reach them in person or by phone.
So here I am.
My stuff at home
My childhood passing me by
Wanting to get better
But here I sit and cry.
I wish someone would listen.
I wish someone would make things right.
Life inside these facilities
Growing up here is just not right.
I want to ride that new bike.
I want to open that new toy.
I want to wear my new clothes.
I want my life to have JOY.—

Listen to the Heart

Words don't always come out,
In the form of simple sound
Words aren't always spoken,
Sometimes, just look around.
The sun can't speak in words.
Communication is in light and heat.
Sometimes it's quiet hiding behind the clouds.
Giving shade for cool retreat
To me my child is like the sun
Radiant and bright
Speaking words may not be there.
But look in her eyes, find her voice.
It is there you see the light.
My child's smile has more meaning.
Though some may not understand
She tells me she loves me with her face.
The sparkle and glow are grand.
Then there are days the sadness,
For her she cannot express
It comes out in severe frustration.
Anger seeming to regress!
The days she is quiet,
Taking it all in.
I wonder what she is thinking,
Behind that silly grin.
Take words for granted,
It is something I cannot do.
My baby cannot talk to me,
The way I talk to you.

I long to hear her thoughts,
Her secrets and her dreams.
But I have learned to be content,
With the sounds of her expressive screams.
Regardless of communication
My heart beats outside my chest.
Autism may steal her words,
But to me she is still the best
As I sit beside her bed
Looking at her sweet face
I am thankful for another day,
Full of love and grace—

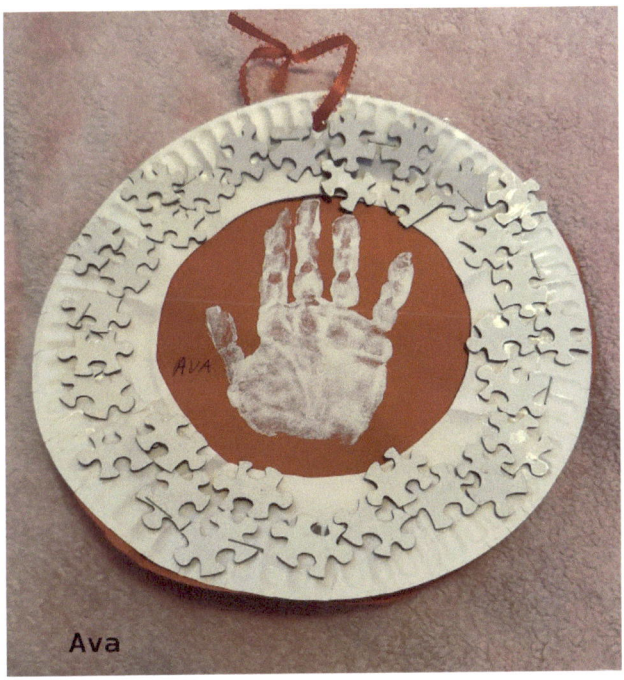

Artwork done by Ava at age 5

Desperately RAD

Constant feeling of desperation
Seemingly, No hope of reparation
Every verbal mental jab
Every painful physical stab
Spewing hate
Always instigate.
Trying to turn the tables
Calling people to come
Crying for help
Yet all that you speak are fables.
Reactive Attachment is what they call it.
Being the target is where I stand.
Being abused every minute by all of this demand
If the wind blows slightly and you do not like it
Its straight into furious mode
If you expect an outcome that doesn't go your way
Take cover, it is about to explode!
They say be understanding.
Be calm and be gentle.
What they do not understand is they are just instrumental
Its feeding the fire and anger inside
The one taking this child on a hellacious ride.
Instead of finding a solution.
Disarming the war
Taking the child on a power trip tour
Its ripping our families to shreds.
It's tearing us apart its ultimately breaking a multitude of hearts! —

Peace Somewhere?

Long days, long nights, tears, heartache, exhaustion, complete draining of every ounce of your being leaves you feeling helpless and almost hopeless. Trying to find even a speckle of hope when things just look so bleak.

Deep breath, close your eyes and inhale slowly and breathe out again. Grasp for whatever you have to get through the next second of this experience. People trying to say to use this method to cope or this skill to calm. Mind so fuzzy and overcome with emotion, just cannot seem to get a hold on and just can feel the entire world about to explode for the 10th time, today.

Emotions taking over so much it feels like the only outlet is to lash out in anger and painful feelings on the inside. I do not know why it gets aggressive and out of control.

Feeling intense on the inside but lost in the moment but can hear that quiet voice deep down trying to help it to calm. How to bring it to the surface so it can calm, how to make that voice louder than the sudden bursts of emotion that get to the mind.

Holds, restraints, locked rooms, is it really helping or just making me feel worse? Trying to stop. Yet it cannot seem to get there .... do not give up, the ability is in there somewhere ... help find why and how to be listening to the stable voice speaking too softly ... help find words that spark peace. Speak peace ...

Spin

This merry go round is anything but fun.
The emotional ups and downs
Not knowing from minute to minute
Can I do this? Can I run?
A smile, a hug, an I love you.
Immediately followed by rage
Can't seem to release the anger inside.
The brain is a crippling cage.
Getting lost in my head.
Can't seem to be free.
Trying to settle but
There is so much in me.
Please mommy I can't stop,
I am trying but I feel so lost.
If you get weary and tears fill your soul
You have been fighting the battle for so long.
I am tired too, my heart feels sad.
I try hard not to be bad.
I hope that they know the drugs that she did have made us pay
a lifetime cost.
The moments I am clear,
As you can see
I am really worth fighting for
So, I can be me.
I know it is hard to see through the hurt.
But know every minute.
I look at your face.
God is giving you a special kind of grace.—

Eyes

Can't quite figure out
What's going on?
Your fine one minute
The next one your gone.
The look in Your eyes
Goes from sparkling to blank.
My heart was unsure while my stomach sank.
You fight so hard, and nobody knows what's in your head.
You stomp and you hit all you see is red.
The bright blue eyes and the pretty blonde hair
Go from adorable to a blank angry stare.
How can we reach you?
You cannot seem to say.
How can we communicate somehow?
Some way.
Oh, sweet little lady,
Blue eyes and blonde hair
I know that you are in there, sweetheart, somewhere!—

Swearing

Calling us names
Try to tear us all apart.
Hitting, screaming
Out of control
All it does is break our heart.
The anger
The rage
The lost little child
Where are you? Are you in there?
Spewing words that stab so deep.
We try to help you,
We cannot sleep.
The dread of another day like that
They thought that we are all going to be abused.
The fear and sadness surround my soul.
When we think of the tools we have used
The hate in your eyes, so deep the seer
The words you say.
Are there voices you are hearing that we cannot hear? —

Burnt out!

Night after night with yelling
The tantrums, the anger, the wild unknown
I cannot seem to relax,
Cannot seem to calm you,
911... the other end of the phone
You have punched me and kicked me.
You have hit me and spit at me.
Then in the morning... its mommy, I am sorry.
I am burnt out.
I am tired.
I am sad and I am mad.
I do not know how much longer I can keep the facade.
I smile and laugh; I put on my game face.
But inside my soul you cause pain you cannot erase
I lay in my bed whenever I can.
I cry myself to sleep.
To quiet my head.
Another whole battle you gave us tonight.
Another whole battle, I am losing my fight.
Your face filled with anger.
Your mouth spewing hate
My heart broken once again.
Day after day
Today, my children as I put feet on the floor.
I cannot even wait to get out of the door.
Dropping you off for six hours of school,
It is my time to reflect to rewind my spool.
My brain is exhausted; my body is tired.
You are draining my heart that once was inspired.

When you get out of bed,
And say it again.
Mommy, I'm sorry.
Mommy, I am sorry.
It feels like my ears are getting deaf.
Your sorry means nothing today to me
Please just be quiet and let me be.
I am trying to gather my brain bit by bit,
Before I end up in the hospital for losing MY shit!—

Stuck

I'm stuck inside my thoughts again.
Can't seem to calm my brain.
I just keep repeating myself,
Please Someone stop the pain.
How can I tell you what is happening inside?
When my mind is stuck in this place
How can I tell you I cannot stop?
I want my brain out of this space.
Can someone please listen?
And with intent
To help get my words out right
Can someone please help me?
Slow down my thoughts I need things clear in my sight.
The times when I'm spinning,
Can't seem to slow down.
This feeling so lonely,
Feel like I could drown!
 Help turn my disparity,
Into sweet clarity,
Let's get my mind to release.
I need help to get ahold of my thoughts.
So, my brain can get some sort of peace.
Speak to me softly,
Speak to me calm.
Hold my hand, hug me tight.
As much as I try to push you away.
I need you to help win this fight.
When my mind gets clear,
My brain gets calm.

I can Thank you for helping me rest.
I will say it to you one more time.
You always look out for my best! —

Art by Rachel age 16

Overload

So many topics rush through my mind.
Running around everyday
So many projects, so many demands
Some days I just want to run away.
Waking up to demands from my 10-year-old son.
Wanting all kinds of things
If his needs are not met immediately
A major tantrum is what he will bring.
Starting my day like this makes me so tired.
Feeling so weary and drained
The mental health issues take over his mind.
His eyes glaze over.
The violence begins then watching my son get restrained.
Why does this happen?
Why is this so hard?
Why can't he just calm himself down?
Take some deep breaths,
Sometimes it takes hours to rest.
His staff is by his side.
Always giving their best.
How can we reach you in these distant times?
How can we help you?
What do you need?
There are no reasons, no rhymes.
I'm just exhausted, my mind will not slow down.
So here I sit at 3am,
Thinking and mulling around
We all try to help you.
While hearing your cries

What could you be thinking,
behind those confused eyes?
There is nothing I want more than to help calm you down.
Help change your little heart to a smile.
Not a frown
So many topics run through my head.
Trying to figure what makes you see red.
It must be so scary when your brain gets so stuck.
Hoping each time, it happens
We have some good luck.
Please know when you're broken and losing control,
I love you always from the depths of my soul!—

Abstract depiction of rage, Lucy, age 15

Miss J

The judge says mom is ready.
You all know she is not!
The judge says just make me go.
It is breaking my heart.
When I was an infant, they took me away.
She could not take care of me.
Now here we are six years later.
Make me visit, I have no say,
With tears in my eyes
My heart is broken.
They want to give me to her.
As some sort of token
The judge doesn't care about the damage she is doing.
They want to pull me from those who've been there.
They show up to take me.
They bring me to her.
All she worries about are the knots in my curly hair.
I am much more than a showpiece for parading around.
I have wit, I have sass, I have smarts, and I care!
Just because they say so, they want me to go.
breaking the laws set for me.
To prove a point, to who?
I'm a six year, can't they see
I have love, I have dreams, I have a heart, and a mind,
Even at six I understand.
The judge in the bench is making a mess.
Everyone is taking a stand.
Please, my life is at stake,
My future uncertain

I cry every time that they say,
The lady is here to take me to her.
This fear is not fair, in the heart of a child.
Dear Judge, please listen to reason.
I am not a pawn.
For me this is not just a season
We are fighting for my life!
We are fighting for me!
Not to be a statistic,
When you bang that gavel
I pray that you can think,
A whole lot more realistic!—

Days

Physically exhausted
Emotionally drained
Mentally wasted.
Rest unattained
Every day
More of the same
We wake up to more drama.
Feeling insane
Trying your coping skills
Give you your med.
But my God little lady
What's happening in your head?
Looking for optimism
Looking for change
looking only to see it even more strange.
Your face looks so empty.
Your happy spunk seems so far away.
Where are you?
Who are you going to be today?
What level
Of difficulty is it going to be?
Listening?
Fighting, or aggressive to me?
Getting so weary
You must be too.
Always so teary, not just me... YOU!
Where did our smiles go?
How about our joy?
What about your laughter?
Your favorite toy?

They call it autism, they call it delay, they call it behavioral, they have so much to say.
This is the baseline.
This is what you get.
What they don't understand is
We keep looking for you.
We have not given up yet!
Diagnosis cannot define and WONT overcome love.
You were created for wonderful things.
From the Father above! —

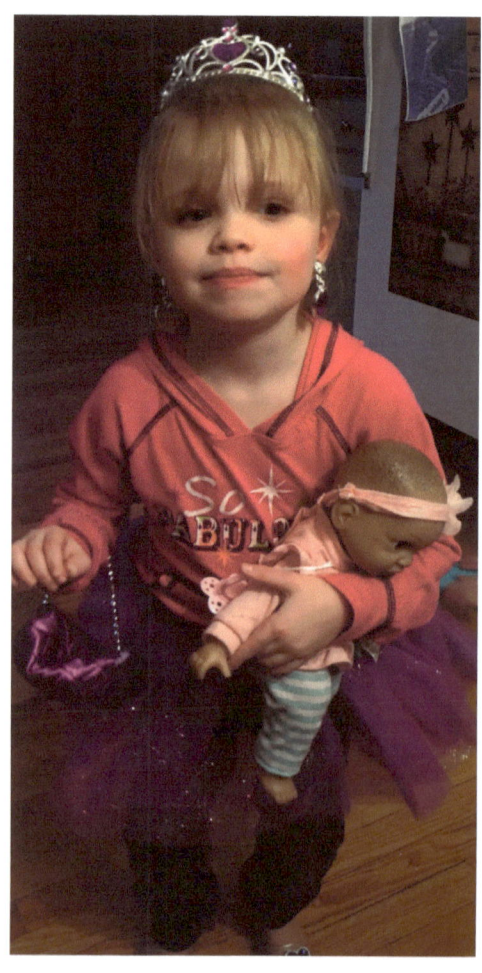

Owen

Bullying and ignorance
Mental health needs
Kids who are different
Work at different speeds
Anger and hate.
Mean words cutting deep.
Sadness overtaking a child awake,
even asleep
Thoughts that race in a child's mind
should not go so dark.
The pain that hurts a child's heart
from just one
cutting mean remark
Understanding challenges that other people face
Treating them with kindness, compassion, and grace
The mean and ugly treatment that is happening everywhere.
The zero-tolerance policy
To bullies please beware.
The behavior needs to stop right now!
Learn and be a better friend.
Together one by one let's bring hatred to an end! —

How?

Trapped inside my little head.
Emotions swirling, seeing red.
Coping skills are not helping me.
I get so anxious, I cannot see.
Biting and banging, spitting in your face,
Hitting and swearing, I'm stuck in this space.
Please make it stop, help me calm down.
I want to take deep breaths, turn over my frown.
I'm trying so hard, peace seems far away.
One breath, now two,
Inhale this way.
Exhale, again to find calm in my soul.
I want to be healed so I can be whole.
So, people please know, that I may need some time.
I'm trying so hard to calm my swirling mind!
Patience is needed, speak calmly to me.
Help me relax my mind, so my smile can be!—

Artwork done by William Barboza, age 17
Follow this artist on Facebook at Willfully Artistic

Emotion

Dazed
Empty
Angry
I quit.
Selfish
Mean
Violent
Lies
Abusive
Rage
Physical
Stage
Lying
Pain
Spiteful
Drain
Intrusive
Instigate
Stubborn
Manipulate
Endless
Intense
Fake
Defense
Accusations
Broken
Twisted
Insanity misspoken.
Chronic
Misplaced Hate
Mental illness

Alienate
Exhausted
Shell
Constant
HELL!!!!!!—

Art by Rachel, age 16

5

Children's Behavioral Health

LOBSTER

I'm going to call this lesson from the lobster! You know how a Lobster is a scavenger; it goes around eating and growing and thriving only to be thrown in a pot to be (IN MY OPINION) one of the most delicious meats there is. the delicious, tender melt in your mouth yumminess.

Well, let's think back to the cooking process. A lobster is placed in a pot of cold water. Then placed on the stove on low heat, this will slowly relax said lobster to eventually fall asleep and be totally oblivious to the fact that they are being cooked. It is being deceived into thinking it is in a good place and slowly as the heat is given...it has no idea the fate it is about gain. It is not thrown screaming into a pot of boiling water; It is slowly desensitized to the things around as it is lulled to sleep. This is how humans' beings are... lulled to sleep by the things we hear every day. We are desensitized by the media, by our friends, by the things we have now become numb to!!! To the things that are true, We don't listen! To the things that are lovely, and just fair. We turn our cheek. We thrive on the drama and the things we hear and read instead of weighing the truth for ourselves. Why do we allow ourselves to be slowly cooked and be totally unaware of things that are important???? I don't want to be lulled to sleep, I want to be very aware and pay close attention to things I am taught, told and things I just know from my conscience are true!!! Get out of the pot!!! Don't be a lobster, think for yourself, listen to your conscience instead of what the noise of the world is trying to convince you is truth.

Services

My teacher asked a question related to my life and advocacy for children with behavioral, emotional, mental health issues, and medically compromised children. While the prompt stated, "which things go hand in hand toward making the healthcare system a success," the process is almost a never ending merry go round of which came first the chicken or the egg.

In order to get access, you must first be able to handle the cost. If the cost is manageable, then there is the question of the quality of the help you need. If the quality is there, is it affordable? Does insurance cover it? Can I access this service? How long is the actual waitlist for accessing services? The wheel continues to spin.

In my own experience, because I have state medical for my adopted kids, I get a lot of things covered that private insurances may not. I do not have co-pays for the children. However, Access is a HUGE issue. Waitlist after waitlist. The cost is analyzed by the provider; it is then determined if they will accept our coverage. If they accept our coverage, it then becomes, how many actual service hours are for the kids? How many are for administrative?

I have been going in circles for a long time speaking to people in authority, trying to make changes so our children get better life outcomes.

I have experienced high quality staff who get paid minimally to do very hard jobs. I have seen and experienced less than quality individuals do the same tasks, getting the same rate of pay as those who work really hard. Cost effective services, quality staff, accessibility all need work, actually they need an overhaul.

They need a forum of parents who experience the services to sit in on the reform process. Our feedback and ideas are crucial for the development of programs, resources and treatments for our children. We don't get the benefit of punching out at 5 O'clock. We live it 24/7. Our voices should matter. Making a difference for the future of our kids long-term!

Thank You,

Potholes to Pavement

As many of us have struggled through this mental health crisis with our loved ones, the analogy of the pothole seemed so fitting.

The water filled hole that looks safe to drive over, yet causes major damage to our vehicle.

Compare that to insufficient services given to people who struggle significantly with some very difficult issues.

The photo at the top of the page of potholes to pavement shows the placement of orange cones. These cones are placed around areas of potential hazard, a way for us to predict a potential danger or mishap.

So many times, with our loved ones don't have the ability to use orange cones, they don't see the signs of a breakdown, they don't know a pothole is coming and they are about to hit it full force.

As a mom, of several children who suffer significantly through no fault of their own with severe mental illness, I am trying to learn to watch for the orange cone, or the antecedent to whatever causes the hitting of the pothole... this time!

Learning to be aware at all times of potential hazard, trying to avoid potholes is something we all as families wish to achieve.

Together we can support each other and be there to navigate nonsense, find the warning signs, however subtle, or loud they may be! May we be there to help each other along the journey to the pavement!

Let's find an open road and celebrate the journey, rejoicing in the victories, both large and small!

Ring that bell

Scaling walls, climbing rocks, trying to find your footing while dangling and struggling through the difficult journey through Children's Behavioral Health. Almost making it to the top to ring the bell, when the rocks are all if a sudden missing from under your feet. Did you really gain any ground? Was there really enough time to find or be taught the strategies needed to produce maximum results? Did the rocks get smaller and suddenly disappear from view leaving you dangling from the top with fear and anxiety about what the next steps should be?

That is how it feels to parent a child with behavioral, emotional, and mental health needs. Services are needed; they are put in place for a very small season only to disappear when progress begins. This leaves children and families left to decide how do we move forward.

Repeated hospitalizations, a revolving door to yet another clinician, who, once again needs to hear the dirty laundry about your child. Usually this takes place in front of them.

Watching your child's face sink just a little more with every word. Asking for navigation through a system of unknown destinations.

Fragmented care... usually frustrating not only the parents, the care givers, the professionals, but more importantly the child who is struggling minute by minute to figure out why? How?? When?? How high do I have to climb?? Will you still be there at the top? Will you stand at the bottom and help me navigate so that one day I can ring the bell of success.

Continuum of care with quality individuals who are paid their worth needs to be a real thing. It needs to not only exist but be functional. There are some fantastic individuals out there trying to do just that. They too, are climbing the wall trying to find the next rock to move to.

They too are trying to scale the wall looking for success and be able to ring the bell of success!

As a parent of multiple children, some biological, some adopted through the foster care system, it can be very challenging and hard to find where your next steps are. Who do we call? How do we access stable, qualified individuals and be able to help our children succeed. Tears, frustration, exhaustion, and hurdle after hurdle we climb. We also scale the wall looking for the same things. Rocks on the way up crumble under our feet and we are set back yet again!

How do we find success? How do we cut the violence in schools? How do we work with prison overload? How do we deal with opiate and drug crisis? How can we ensure Whole Child?

While the answer is so simple, it is also quite complicated.

We need to address these needs early on! Why wait until the whole neighborhood is on fire when we could have extinguished the spark early on!

Let's get our children what they need and deserve... whole life, climbing walls of success not adversity. Let's teach our children that the rocks we climb, while we will be met with both success and challenges. They have solid tools and skills to climb to the top and RING THAT BELL!

The Room

Going into mediation
Books lining all the walls
Polished wood
Duty calls
Sitting around an antique table
Looking to gain insight
Talking about the issues
Vulnerable children are why we fight
What do we need
How can we attain
Talking about solutions
To fix the broken chain
So many links
So much rust
So much damage
So much distrust
If we work together
Join each link holding strong
If we work together
To move things along
The time is now
To clean the chain
Expose it to sunshine
Get it out of the rain
People have suffered
Families broken
Services missing
Yet many words are spoken
It's time to put feet on plans made for so long

Rebecca Almeida

It's time to correct things that have gone so wrong
Generational madness
Cycles repeat
Services still missing
Families in defeat
Joining our arms
Raising our voices
Changing the systems
Giving families choices
When broken links get replaced
The rust is cleaned off
Helping families
Rebuilding trust
Leaving mediation
Hope is in sight
Please don't stop working
We must win this fight!
When we think of the task
And what we must do
Remember the families
Are just like me and YOU!
Hold onto the hope
Don't put it to rest
Remember their faces
Let's give it our best—

6

Letters

What is My Why?

I was just sitting here doing school and it occurred to me I was dealing with one of my triplets that I adopted who was having a severe tantrum after dinner. We had to call rescue because he would not settle, and the self-injurious behaviors were pretty intense!

As I am sitting here reflecting on my day and my stress level between that and having to write a paper for my class on something that bores me to tears... I thought this thought... why? Why am I here and dealing with all this? Why is this kid having to deal with the consequences of choices made by his mother aka incubator... drugs, alcohol...on and on... why does this class want me to analyze the political parts of healthcare and the lack of spending in social services, why is the disability trend rising and nobody wants to talk about the real issue.

Well, if you survived my rant... here is what I think ... why? Because I have a job to do. I have to take care of this child and love him to the other side of the hellacious hand he was dealt. Why do I have to write about things that infuriate me like political blah blah blah when my heart screams for common sense to be used by the people who can control it!

Then... I apply it to my health! I have a mouth and a gift to advocate. I have to learn to channel that and gain more insight into the things that can change the course of sail for so many... including me!

Eating healthy, making good choices, moving my body and getting things done for ME! I need to get healthy for ME! To have the energy to raise these children entrusted to me! I need to be healthy and have the energy and knowledge it takes to pour into lives and make changes! So why??? Simple yet complicated ME!

What's your why today???

Happiness is Colors

I have struggled to think of what happiness meant to me. There have been so many struggles that are serious in my life. I have been internally questioning whether true happiness existed or if it was just a state of mind that lasts for a season. The rug of life has been ripped out from under me so many times in the past year. Stress and sadness have had the tendency to cloud my ability to find happiness. Then a friend said to me that my happiness is colors. A light turned in in my head. Colors always bring me to a place of happiness,

Today, I received a phone call that would once again shake my world and the lives of people I love, to the core. My 25-year-old niece passed away in the late morning. She was like one of my own children for a season. She had a hard life growing up and suffered many losses throughout her time on earth. She chose to mix herself up with drugs. She chose to color her world with substances to numb the pain. She chose to mix red for anger. Living with color black and walking in the darkness of pain that held her captive. She made choices in colors that did not represent happiness.

We all start with a white canvas in which the colors of life are given to us to create our artwork. We are all given brushes and a vast amount of choices in colors to begin and continue the masterpiece God created us to be. With each stroke of the brush an event has made an impression. With every application of the colors to the canvas a new piece is reaching potential to be amazing. The red I choose represents the fire in my heart, the burning I feel to help people attain their full ability and blossom. Green brings new life, allowing for a backdrop for other colors to shine. The blue for me is freedom to be me. Freedom to express my heart and be heard. The yellow is bright and cheer. Yellow sun shining on my face and making me warm. Then there are times that pinks, purples and oranges are created by mixing experiences with others. These colors really make an impact on me because they mean that lives have interacted and left lasting impressions.

My heart is full and happiness in full blossom when I use color all around me. Happiness to me is allowing my canvas to be painted with a wide array of shades of colors. Happiness is colors forming impressions, making impacts on people. Making the canvas beautiful.

There are colors given to all of us in life. How we choose to use them is our choice. When obstacles are put in our path, we have choices to make on application. I am choosing to allow the colors to continue to bring happiness into my world.

Watching

For years now, I have watched from the sidelines and thought to myself, if only I could take this weight off, If only I could get myself to like exercise (self-professed allergy for years) If only I could find the magic pill that could melt this fat off me. I would buy the People magazine edition every time they ran the Half My Size stories. I would look through and read the stories and think...ugh I guess I can't do this. Then....this year happened. People took a chance and got some guts to tell me what I needed to hear, with love and gentleness and a passive aggressive subtle kick in my behind that I needed. If people didn't care enough to take a chance...I would still be 64 lbs. heavier, I would still be sitting here day after day watching TV and letting life pass me by! I would still be out of breath walking from the couch to the refrigerator and back to feed this obesity again and again. If people didn't take a risk and think maybe I can help her..., Where would I be??? My life has changed because of a person who took a risk....my life continues to change because of each of you. You wouldn't have caught me dead at a piYo class or the gym, you wouldn't have seen my carriage at the grocery full of healthy choices. I still get to the checkout belt and giggle to myself at the difference in my shopping! So, if you're sick of sitting on the sidelines and dreaming about change, it's time to do something for YOU! Stop watching from the sidelines and start living!

Realization

Every action you take is a vote for the person you want to become Well after sitting in Therapy today, I realized my brokenness and need to be accepted and need to help everyone around me no matter what it is doing to my own mind, heart and soul. I have realized that my boundaries are missing in an effort to make sure everyone has everything, and I have depleted my own supply of self-worth, self-esteem, I am lied to, disrespected, talked about behind my back, and basically people think I'm oblivious to that. I am not! I'm hurt! I'm tired. I'm sad, I am broken! I get taken advantage of regularly by people who claim to love me. But behind my back make claims that I am not doing things in their best interest.

I have advocated, fought, and put my heart on the line so many times.

I can't do it anymore! I just can't. I'm sick of feeling like I failed. I look at the facts in front of me and see the fruit of my labor and to me I guess I failed.

I have been called a bitch, I have been told I'm hated, I have been accused of hating, I have been accused of malicious taking of money, I have been accused of to take control of things that aren't mine.

I am so hurt. My therapist said I am like a battered wife trying to fix everything for everyone else in hopes it will help fix my broken heart.

I have made a ton of mistakes in my life. I have done a ton of stupid things and I'm sorry for that. I hope you can forgive me, At the same time, I hope you can self-reflect and stop hurting yourselves and others.

7

Addiction

Fence Post

Digging holes deep in the dirt
Burying years of disappointment and hurt
With every shovel full of rocks and soil,
All really heavy just like the turmoil
Putting on a tough face
Don't let many people see
That inside this hard shell is vulnerable me
Hiding myself like a hard wooden post
Placing it deep in the hole
much like the pain inside of my heart,
The hurt still wearies my soul
Once the posts have set deep down in the ground
making sure nobody will see
Attaching tall panels
Connecting the pain, hiding some more,
can't see me!
As time has gone on and the fence starts to weather, the pain comes to the surface again
Covering it up with paint or by sanding
another temporary fix to keep the fence standing
But the fence man knows to make sure
That the fence stands up tall and secure
The fence man knows what needs to be done-to make sure the fence is sturdy
And all of the weather endured
Mr. fence man, it's time to clean the hole correctly
To make room for a brand-new post
Mr. fence man you know
The new fence will be so much better
To make your life ... the most!—

Not without Hope

Overwhelmed
Broken
Tired
Words so sweet words unspoken
Spinning plates
All at once
Each holding fragile parts
Tired arms
Tired mind
Tired broken hearts
Everything seems to get harder
Answers are so far away
The struggles we have
Get more difficult than we face another day
Keeping plates spinning
Try putting some down
But if we slow down or let ourselves stop
Can't let that happen can't let them drop
Hopeless feeling
Helpless, reeling
Stop, breathe remember when

You held the hand of Jesus
You knew he would never leave
He is standing waiting
Ask him to help you stand
All the things you're trying
Keep bringing you back to where you land
When you stood in the lake

Just Another Tuesday

Remember what you said
I give my life to Jesus
By Him I will be led.
The pain and all the heartbreak
The ache so deep inside
He has His hand stretched out to you
Grab on
stop believing the lies
You are worth it
You are loved
You are not without hope
The one you need is Jesus
It doesn't come from Dope!—

What Do They Know

Started defeated
Years, I didn't care
Got me to this place
Depression
Anxiety
Hopelessness
Despair
Looked in a mirror
Don't recognize me
Broken and weighed down
No energy
Searching and reaching
Trying to control my addictions
Can't seem to put down the drug
In spite of my convictions
Food is a necessity
For me it is a drug
You cannot just eliminate it
Or walk away and shrug
There are choices
I have to make
Conscious of the Consequences
Before I partake
Trying to numb the pain
With chips, chocolate or ice cream
Only helps for a minute
Like heroin or cocaine
While it may not be illegal
This addiction is just as real

Eating stuff in excess
Try not to feel
Then pound by pound
Pain by pain
Self esteem
Down the drain
BUT...
reach within
Find your voice
Know that YOU
Have a choice
Take a step
Then take two and three
Find food that gives you what you need
Build strength, get energy
You are worth it
Don't listen to the lies
Your beautiful inside and out
Look at yourself through Gods eyes
He loves you as you are
Each and every day
Hold His Hand, and ask Him
To show you the way
Step by step
As you were designed
Health and Wellbeing
in your soul, body and your mind—

STARTLED

Woke up just now in a cold sweat
Thinking about you and all the regret
I'm scared beyond words
I'm scared to my core
I pray every minute
For you to come through the door
Asking for help
And for a fresh start
To beat all these habits that are ripping you apart
Losing so much one thing at a time
It makes no sense
No reason, no rhyme
Please my sweet baby who turned into a man
Let us get you the help you need
Let's make a new plan
Your prides in the way
But my dear boy, nothing else matters
Watching you struggle....
My heart shatters!
So here I lay in bed in the middle of the night
Awake in a cold sweat
Awake in real fright
I love you my baby turned into a man
Let's get over this addiction
Do all That we can
Stop making excuses
Stop lying to all
This monster is bigger
It's making you fall

You're bigger
You're stronger, I know that you can
Where is my sweet baby, who turned into a man—

8

Grief

Roller Coaster Ride

This pretty much sums up the last 10 years of my life! Grief is so hard to put into words and so hard to process every day!

There are days when I feel like I am climbing up this very tall slope... waiting to get to the top of the trial and unaware of what the top will hold for me, the climb is exhausting, and I often feel winded.

When the storm seems to settle and things go back to somewhat of a normal life (if there is such a thing) I arrive at the top of the hill and can see for miles and things are clear.

Then all of a sudden, the next thing is the uncertain ride down the hill...steep...twisting even some upside-down time where everything seems to be all over the place,

There are days when I feel like I am going down the hill at top speed and the safety belt comes undone!

I scream... I cry in fear.... hold on tight and trust that it will all settle in a minute when the straightaway comes up at the bottom of the turn! Uncontrolled ....

I had so much success in my life change and my embracing of plan B when my journey as a mom began almost 34 years ago. The struggle with weight grew and grew and I found myself so unhealthy and unhappy. That seemed like a very steep uphill climb until I was starting to see the top of the hill, the success and the way I was feeling with energy and working out and eating healthy. I was at the top of the hill looking out and things were feeling pretty good!

Then Trauma took me on the downhill trip. What was about to happen threw me completely off the track!! My old habits crept in; my depression and fear hit an all-time high...my search for the track was so clouded by the grief and pain I had in my heart and mind. The amount of responsibility is overwhelming...I couldn't find the track it was lost in the trees and my heart and mind and ME got lost for what felt like a never-ending season....reckless, broken, sad, and alone in rooms full of people....ME, trying to embrace my new normal!

I met a friend who got my struggle with my weight and understood my insecurities that I try so hard to hide behind my smile and my joking... this person spoke into my life without realizing the impact it had on my heart. This person told me that I am beautiful and my eyes filled up and tears ran down my face because the brokenness I have been feeling left me feeling anything but beautiful in my heart and mind. And yet, I knew it was genuine....as the tears fell down my cheeks, they were wiped away by someone who really cared.

My ride was located....my journey restarting and I have found my motivation. I have found the hill to climb...I'm afraid yet somewhere inside is the fearless girl who can do anything she puts her mind to!

Grief is real and manifests itself in many forms and is different for everyone...there is no time line and no way grief should occur.....it's different and painful and hard! but.....Thanks to the people who hold me and know my struggle with weight and telling me positive things so I can believe in myself again for the first time in a long time! Hard truth but I need to always be honest and accountable!!! Much love to all!

GRIEF

When someone dies
The world still spins.
People still
Move on with their lives.
How can you keep moving,
like nothing has happened.
My loved one has left me.
I'm left here with the pain.
My heart is shattered.
My brain could explode.
My stomach feels nausea.
I can't handle this load.
The pain, and the emptiness
It won't go away.
I'm so overwhelmed.
I can't even pray.
I sit and I stare, with tears on my face.
Trying to make sense of this empty space.
How can I move on?
I cannot really think.
My eyes burn from emotions.
Its hurts when I blink.
The world around me moves in slow motion.
With everyone around me
In seeming commotion.
Do they not know?
Do they not care?
My world has shifted,
Beyond repair.

Don't ask me if I am ok.
Obviously, the answer is no.
How can I be, ok?
I didn't want them to go.
Give me give me some time.
Give me some space!
This hurt is so deep.
My memories I will embrace.
In the meantime, if you see me,
Don't ask what to do.
Just hug me tight,
And love me through!—

Sleeping

Perfect little guy
Born sleeping.
Eyes closed.
We ask why.
Perfect little face
Lots of dark hair
Tiny little mouth
This just isn't fair.
Perfect little lips
Chubby little cheeks
Mommy and Daddy waited for you for over 38 weeks.
Long little fingers and long little toes
Tiny little ears and a sweet button nose
When you arrived sleeping
To a room full of tears
The tears were a mixture of love sadness and fears.
God has a plan for you.
We may never understand why.
But God needed you for a special job.
Because you're a special guy
Colson, this is so hard.
Please ask God to give Special grace.
Until the day we see you again
And kiss your beautiful face. —

My Angel

God chose me.
He gave me a gift.
It grew in my womb.
I was so excited.
Even prepared a room.
My heart and arms were prepared to embrace.
To love and to raise that sweet little face.
I felt every kick.
I felt every wiggle.
But oh, how longed to just hear you giggle.
Gods plan for you was one I did not see.
When it was time for you to arrive
God said, you are my angel, come right to me.
The tears and the pain that is felt in my soul.
I don't know if I will ever feel whole.
But God knew when He chose me to be this child's mother.
He knew I would nurture like no other.
He had a plan we just couldn't see, when God told our angel, Come right to Me! —

One Last

Walking in the room
Daddy hands you to me.
I kiss your sweet face.
It's as cold as could be.
My eyes fill up.
With you on my arm,
the tears well up
Yet I feel a strange calm.
Gazing down, can't stop my tears.
Thinking about missing all your years
Telling you stories, playing a song,
Trying so hard to keep strong.
My sweet little grandson
You taught me so much.
In just the few hours
We got to touch.
You taught me what it means to hang on so tight.
When pain hurts so much all day and all night.
You taught me to be there despite my fear.
To be the real me and release every tear.
To not be afraid to let them all out.
It's what loving you so much is what it's about.
You taught me that daddy has so much to love.
His tender heart for mommy and for God above
Together to honor your life every day
To support each-other in every way
When times get hard
And they feel really sad.
Remind us, sweet Colson, of the love that we had.

Move one step forward.
One step every day
The love all around
Will show us the way. —

My Sweet Colson

Started off today going to get ready for you.
Lots of dinosaurs, fun toys, and books for me to read.
Making sure your room looked cute.
So, you had everything you would need.
We have all have been so excited to see your sweet face.
But I'm going to tell you a secret little grandson.
Mimi wanted to take you everyplace.
I have thought about you and dreamed how much I've loved you from the start.
How could such a little man have stolen my whole heart.
I thought about the stroller and taking you for long walks.
I thought about your first words.
I thought of our funny talks.
I dreamt of baking cookies.
Putting chocolate on your nose
I dreamt of taking off your sock and smelling little toes.
I thought of you sitting on my lap and rocking you as you rest.
I thought about you falling asleep on me, that feeling was the best.
I dreamt of the day you called my name and asked me to come and play.
I thought about how we could go, and I would do anything you say.
McDonalds to the playland,
Chuck e cheeses for some games,
the zoo to see the animals,
the places I thought and dreamt about,
are too many to name.
Instead, my sweet little grandson,
God needed you for a special task.
He called you home before we could do any of the things we ask.
There are so many here that love you,

so many here that mourn.
Mommy and Daddy,
please send them a sign that you're ok.
Please send them peace each and
every day.
But as for me, sweet Colson, forever in my heart,
I will love you always, just like from the start.
I will not stop dreaming if all we could have done,
It will just be different now,
You are always my baby, my sweet grandson! —

Artist is Kortney, age 13

One Week

One week ago, today
I saw your little face.
One week ago, today
It was our first embrace.
One week ago, today
My eyes filled up with tears.
Realizing that moment
That this fulfilled my fears
Your little face was perfect.
Your hands were so small.
Your toes so long,
Your cuter than all!
As I held you close
I told you just how loved you are.
To me you are greater than the sun, the moon, or even the biggest star
You're the first to make me a Mimi
The first to steal my heart.
You're with me still, every day.
Even though we are far apart. —

The Ride

Time has both flown by and dragged all at the same time! We are doing ok! Life seems to just go on around us and so like being on a highway you have to move with the flow! If you stop, you will get run over and if you go too fast somehow you will get a ticket and force you to just flow with life! Trying to flow and not get in the wrong lane or on the wrong side of the highway! Not easy let me just tell you! My car contains a lot of responsibility, and I have to make life work for us! People have voiced opinions and judged me for my response, but you know what.... Until you have driven this car.... You have no clue how hard it can be... Some days trying to flow with the traffic with a flat tire and no transmission fluid... Hard to steer and rough ride! But I'm trying to flow... Every once in a while, I have to pull into a rest stop and refill and get some help with my ride! To my friends who are riding this with me... I love you!! To the ones who don't know what to say to me... It's ok ... I'm still me and I am not made of porcelain!! Love to all!!!

Daddy's Heart

On a hot June day
The world changed a lot
Especially for one man
For a little girl would steal his heart
Her first breath, her first scream
Her first smile
Her daddy's dream
From holding her in his arms
to sitting in the chair
From bald little Jessica
To bows in her hair
The love in his eyes
When he heard her giggle
As he bounced her on his knee
The smile in his eyes
This love was meant to be
When Jessica was in the room
The sparkle is his eye
The smile on his face
The deep proud daddy sigh
Always daddy's little girl
from first steps
To watching her grow
Watching her sing and dance and twirl.
When he saw her grow into the woman she is now
The tears rolled down his cheek
He thought about time then he wondered, How
How did this all happen in what felt like a day
But he knew his baby girl in his heart would stay!

Rebecca Almeida

Unexpected, God called him home
Leaving hearts so distraught
But one thing we know
In God's incomprehensible wisdom, His plan He brought
As his baby girl gave birth to her own
First one then two and three
Making him a grandpa
When baby Colson went straight to heaven
Pepere can bounce him on his knee
It doesn't make much sense
The plan we cannot see
God makes a plan
We don't understand why
Sometimes it hurts so deeply
It makes our hearts and soul cry
God too, is her Father
Filled with so much love
Sitting with her daddy in heaven
Watching proudly from above! —

Lady D

Sitting and watching
Holding your hand
Life passes quickly
Hourglass sand
Since you were a young girl
You gave Jesus your heart
Faithful to Him
Nothing tears it apart
Health challenges come on
Things meant to take you down
Met with a song in your soul
Never frown
Mercy you are given
Grace, you display
The Father is waiting
So, He can say
Welcome home Rhoda
Worship will be
Well done faithful servant
You belong to me —

9

SICKNESS

Hope

Doctors say they found more lumps
They have to operate again
Cancer can NOT stop me
Surgery they recommend
Treatment after treatment
Trial after trial
God shows up and walks with me
Every single mile
Life has been a challenge
Battling struggles for so long
But at the end of every day
God gives me a song
The words are not always the same
The meaning always is
I'm not in this fight alone
God will win this game
In moments of weakness
He is my strength
In moments of fear
He goes to every length
Promises He makes
He does not go back
He gives you what you need
You will never lack
When you feel down
About the news that you heard
Cancer is nothing
Trust God at his word —

Proverbs 3:5-6, *"Trust in the Lord with all your heart and lean not on your own understanding; in all your ways submit to him, and he will make poor your paths straight."*
This is dedicated to my friend and true warrior, Mark Rutland, and all the others battling this monster called Cancer! My prayers are with you always!

Mama Blais

Dear Mama
Remember when I grew inside your womb
Remember when you made me a room
Remember when my brothers arrived
Being the best momma
You always strived
Looking back on the memories I love
Thinking back God picked you from above
You held my hand
You hugged me tight, sang me songs, kissed me good night
As time went on
Growing up into a man
God still, He knew He had a plan
The sparkle in your eye
The smile on your face
The love in your heart
No one can erase
While memory seems to have gone far away
My heart still overflows with love tears rolled down my cheeks
When I saw you today
Seeing you look confused and sometimes not knowing
Your sparkle dimmer
Your smile is not glowing
But Mama, you raised me right
You taught me what love is
You showed me how to stand
So even when it gets really hard
I'm here to hold your hand
It may seem you don't remember

But love permeated
You and me, mama, are connected
Because by God we are created
God holds us both in HIS hands
He wiped the tears
He understands
So, mama, hear me with your heart
No matter what
No disease can ever tear us apart
I love you mama!—

10

Sexual Abuse

TRIGGER WARNING

The following poems are about sexual abuse.
They contain very raw content. They are meant to expose
and bring a sense of realization that you are NOT alone!
If you are a victim of sexual abuse, or know someone who is,
please seek therapy. It is very helpful with the right person
helping you process!

Why

Why are we silent
Why do we feel shame
Why aren't the predators called out by name
Why are we embarrassed
Why do we hide
Why do the predators
Stand with such pride
Why are we less than
Why do we accept defeat
All of the predators should be under our feet
The innocence they stole, causing fear and despair
Afraid of everything, everyone, everywhere
Trust is impossible
Self-esteem really bad
Predators holding us
Captive and sad
It's like wearing a robe that is heavy and torn
Walking around feeling hopeless and worn
Taking off this garment piece by tattered piece
Naming each rag ripped off
For relief
Anger
Hate
Disgust
Rage
Oh, there are so many emotions for each piece.
Dirty
Shame
Sadness

Unclean
Rip off more pieces too so I can be seen
Fear
Distrust
No self esteem
That dirty pig has robbed so many dreams
I choose to find freedom
Keep ripping off rags
Until the real me has arrived
So, calling my predator here out by name
Is a start to end his sick twisted game Andrew Hunt
Is a pig
Feel free to name your name
Call out your predator
Don't be afraid to say
Don't let that scum
Take one more second of your day—

Pig

It all came out when I was eight
By that time, I was filled with so much hate
Violated by that disgusting boy
Who tried to use me as his sex toy
His smell still burns fresh in my nose
The scent brings on nausea
from my head to my toes
The Pringles and Pepsi to distract my young brother
He'd put on the TV, for him to watch something or other
His hands were so rough
His eyes are so cold
He did bad things to me
Since I was four years old
Your daddy is paying me to do this to you
So be a good girl, and keep this between us
The babysitter was hurting me
And you had no clue
I know that the emptiness began to fill my soul
As week after week this monster came by
To rape me again, tears rolling down my cheeks, and an intense internal cry
How could you pay him, I don't understand
I thought that you loved me
I thought that you cared

But here we are once again,
Snacks hidden behind the tree
Once again coming to do this to me
The pain, the discomfort, the sadness I feel

As he hurt me one more time
This cannot be real,
This is a nightmare
Disgusting, no reason, no rhyme
It's burning, I told him
He'd tell me to enjoy
The pain was so awful
I was just a sex toy
When it was over, daddy came home
He gave the abuser some cash
Meanwhile, his little girl with tears in her eyes, her heart was starting to crash
The babysitter wanted my friend to join us for one night
I told her that he did that
She put up a fight
Straight to my mommy
She ran and she spoke
My mommy was crying
Her tears made her choke

The fear that I told our dirty little lie
Would I have to still deal with that nasty guy
Never again did he come to the door,
Never again was I held to the floor
The hate and the hurt that he brought to my life
Driving a stake through my heart
My daddy had no idea
He had no clue
But I blamed him from the start
Now that I'm older, the wounds are sometimes raw
Like a scared little girl that's pinned the floor
Nobody can come past where I let you go
I built up thick walls to protect me you know